Leopold Witte, John Thomas Betts

A glance at the Italian Inquisition

A sketch of Pietro Carnesecchi

Leopold Witte, John Thomas Betts

A glance at the Italian Inquisition
A sketch of Pietro Carnesecchi

ISBN/EAN: 9783741177965

Manufactured in Europe, USA, Canada, Australia, Japa

Cover: Foto ©Andreas Hilbeck / pixelio.de

Manufactured and distributed by brebook publishing software (www.brebook.com)

Leopold Witte, John Thomas Betts

A glance at the Italian Inquisition

THE SANBENITO.

A GLANCE

AT THE

ITALIAN INQUISITION.

A SKETCH OF

PIETRO CARNESECCHI:

HIS TRIAL BEFORE THE SUPREME COURT OF THE
PAPAL INQUISITION AT ROME, AND HIS
MARTYRDOM IN 1566.

Translated from the German of Leopold Witte

BY

JOHN T. BETTS.

'By their fruits ye shall know them.'

THE RELIGIOUS TRACT SOCIETY
56 PATERNOSTER ROW, AND 65 ST. PAUL'S CHURCHYARD.
1885.

'However seldom the Tribunal of the Roman Inquisition has been induced to reveal its secrets to anyone, however powerful he might be, and even then but restrictedly, nevertheless, there are instances of processes having been sent to Foreign Courts. Paul IV., most jealous of those secrets, when he sent his nephew, Cardinal Caraffa, to Philip of Spain, sent with him in his suite Girolamo of Nichisola, a Dominican monk, fully informed of the process instituted by that Pontiff against Cardinal Pole, and gave orders that a copy of that process should be handed to them in order that the Cardinal should show it to the King and to his ministers, *a thing quite unusual with the venerated decrees of the Holy Office, but so decreed by the Pope that it should be seen that he did not proceed against that personage under passionate impulse.*

' These words in Italics are found in Bartholomeo Carrara's *Life of Pope Paul IV*. Carrara is styled by Padre Lagomarsini *eruditus ac diligens historicus*, in a note on page 26 of Vol. I. *delle Lettere Poggiane.*'—See Preface to the ' Extract from the Record of the Proceedings against Pietro Carnesecchi,' addressed by Count Manzoni di Lugo to the Reale Deputazione di Storia Patria Italiana.

PREFACE.

THIS little book was published in Germany as one of the many contributions to the literature of the Luther Commemoration of 1883. It deals with the life of a man little known in England, but one who deserves to be held in honoured remembrance by all Protestants. His life is all the more interesting because of his acquaintance with Juán de Valdés and the circle he collected at Naples. The Romish Church condemned these men and women seeking after the true light as heretics, and judged them worthy only of death; but in so doing has enabled us to see the true spirit of Roman Catholicism at the time when it was beginning to lose its absolute sway over Europe. The articles of condemnation in Carnesecchi's case, the statements of belief for which he died, are in almost every instance simple statements of Evangelical truth. The Papacy in condemning him wrote its own condemnation, and made it evident that the high official who claimed to be Christ's Vicar-General on earth was in reality Antichrist himself, alien in thought, in life, and spirit from the Master he professed to serve.

Pietro Carnesecchi was an earnest seeker after the truth. He was the friend and the associate of the most brilliant and the best men and women of his time. He sealed his testimony with his blood, and he died rather than deny the great doctrine of justification by faith. He is a mirror in which we may see what was best in Italian life and thought in the sixteenth century, and in which we may also see what a cruel, pitiless, wholly unchristian system the Italian Inquisition was.

CONTENTS.

CHAPTER I.
INTRODUCTORY 9

CHAPTER II.
CARNESECCHI'S YOUTH AND EARLY LIFE AT ROME 16

CHAPTER III.
INFLUENCE OF JUÁN DE VALDÉS . . . 25

CHAPTER IV.
LIFE IN FLORENCE, VENICE, AND PARIS . . 40

CHAPTER V.
ACCESSION OF PAUL IV. 51

CHAPTER VI.
PERSECUTION UNDER PAUL IV. . . . 58

CHAPTER VII.
REVERSAL OF THE FIRST SENTENCE . . 67

CHAPTER VIII.
THE FINAL TRIAL, ARTICLES OF CONDEMNATION, THE SENTENCE, AND MARTYRDOM OF CARNESECCHI 76

A GLANCE

AT THE

ITALIAN INQUISITION.

CHAPTER I.

INTRODUCTORY.

A HISTORY of the Spanish Inquisition was written in the year 1817 by the Spaniard, Don Juan Antonio Llorente. First as advocate, then as priest, he attained high position in both careers. He occupied himself in clearing up what had transpired in the preceding century, and his task, one imposed by the French Government, then dominant, was a commission to investigate the archives of the Inquisition. When Joseph Bonaparte lost paramount rule in Spain, and after the restoration of Ferdinand VII., bringing in as it did absolute government, the Spanish Inquisition was again re-established, and Llorente incurred, as did other Liberals, sentence of exile. He went to Paris, where, filled with deadly enmity to the Papacy, he wrote the book which, by the publication of important documents, became of permanent interest for the attainment of the knowledge of this, the darkest page in the history of religious fanaticism. Would that some one might some day be able to write the history of the *Roman Inquisition*! There was a time when opportunity presented itself for doing so. The great centraliser, Napoleon I., purposed erecting at Paris a central depôt for the archives of Europe; and toward the close of the year 1809, innumerable waggons carried the records and archives of the German Empire and of other countries to Paris. Even Rome was compelled to reveal her secrets, and from the 27th February, 1810, up to the year 1813, the most secret and the most carefully preserved correspondence, trials, documents, manuscripts, &c., passed from Papal control, beyond the Alps. From the archives of the Vatican there went no less than 45,818 volumes, contained in 3,239 cases, weighing 408,459 kilogrammes.[1] Until the restoration of the Bourbons this immense collection remained in Paris, but science profited little thereby, for access to the collection was prohibited.

Protected by Prussian Grenadiers, and after the fall of the Usurper, the pictures which had been stolen from Florence, and pre-eminently the Vision of Ezekiel, that jewel of Raphael's most brilliant

---

[1] According to Benrath, *Upon the Romish Archives in Trinity College Library*, Dublin, contained in Von Sybel's *Historic Periodical*, 1879, p. 254.

period, were taken down from the walls of the Louvre, and carried back in triumph.[1] Thus the victory of the Allies brought about likewise the restoration of the Romish archives to the Curia. By the month of July, 1817, Louis XVIII. had again delivered up to Pius VII. the invaluable sources of secret Papal history.

In the meanwhile, however, all had not been restored. After the Curia itself, by repeated reclamations, had obtained further deliveries, in the year 1846 Papal documents suddenly turned up in Paris, which were offered by a private individual for sale to the British Museum; but the price he fixed upon them was held to be too high. However, the late Duke of Manchester bought them for £600, and then brought them to London; subsequently he took them over to Ireland. There they were investigated by a clergyman of the Irish Established Church, the Rev. Richard Gibbings, who three times consecutively, in 1852, 1853, and 1856, astonished the world with publications from the original MSS. of the Roman Inquisition, which in themselves undoubtedly bore the stamp of authenticity.

The first intimation given by Mr. Gibbings as to the source whence his originals came was in the third publication, entitled: *Report of the Trial and*

[1] Alfred Von Reumont, *Contributions to Italian History*, 1853. Vol. ii., p. 282.

Martyrdom of Pietro Carnesecchi, sometime Secretary to Pope Clement VII., and Apostolic Protonotary. Transcribed from the original MS. The Duke of Manchester determined to dispose of the records, and he sold them for £500 to the Rev. Richard Gibbings, D.D.—an outlay which possibly trenched upon the latter's means. They were again offered for sale to the authorities of Trinity College, but were finally purchased by the Vice-Provost, Dr. Wall, and by him presented to Trinity College Library, Dublin.

A German scholar, Professor Karl Benrath, of Bonn, who had occupied himself for years with the history of the Italian Reformation, found these valuable records to be, in the year 1876, in a perfectly disordered state, and by way of recognition of the friendly reception given him by the Librarian, he put the fifty-seven bound volumes and the twelve unbound ones into classified order. Fourteen of the comprehensive volumes of the collection contain original Records of the Romish Inquisition, comprising as they do the final judgments of the Inquisition in the trials of Italian heretics, which were given between the 16th December, 1564, and the year 1659, with, however, some intervals. The above-mentioned publication by Gibbings upon Carnesecchi is an instance of a final judgment extracted by the publisher of these documents, in relation to which Professor Benrath judiciously presumed that they are the remains of Papal Records left in Paris in the year 1817.

It would, indeed, be impracticable to write a continuous history of the Romish Inquisition, taking it from these Dublin Records. In the meanwhile, however, they comprise extremely important materials, throwing a clear light upon the reaction to the Reformation, just when it was in its fullest activity. It is possible that other important material may come to hand—as in this instance, which was not only a record of some twenty printed pages, as described by Mr. Gibbings, in the final judgment of Carnesecchi's process—but is also a detailed extract of the whole conduct of the trial.

Count Giacomo Manzoni of Lugo had the good fortune, in the year 1860, to be able to purchase a great portion of the archives of the Dandini family through the bookseller, Guidi, of Bologna. The Dandini family was one whence issued several distinguished prelates, even during the time of the Reformation. This collection likewise contained important documents upon the Reformation movement in Italy during the sixteenth century, and upon the most distinguished persons engaged in it—Flaminio, Cardinal Pole, Donato Rullo, Luigi Priuli, Vittoria Colonna, Cardinal Morone, and others. Manzoni, in order to show what may be expected from these archives for learning and the

Church, has given a specimen, selected from his rich store, of a process, which he printed at Turin in 1870, in a volume which appeared in the 'Miscellanea of patriotic Italian history.' This process was entitled, '*Extract of Pietro Carnesecchi's Trial, which will, in many respects, be probably found to be the most interesting and the most instructive of all the Records of the Inquisition.*'

Manzoni presumes that his documents are the contemporary copy of an extract from the papers of that trial, which the Romish Court itself sent by the hand of its Nuncio at Paris, Cardinal Girolamo Dandini, to Queen Catherine de' Medici, she being Queen of France, and Carnesecchi's patroness. Carnesecchi himself spent several years in Paris subsequently to the year 1547. Catherine retained her friendly feeling for her nephew Cosimo's favourite ; Cosimo being Duke of Florence.

This process brings before us the proceedings of the tribunal of the Inquisition in the most definite and clear manner. We shall in the following pages have an opportunity of witnessing the tactics of the Inquisitors in detail. But the record assumes great importance, for Carnesecchi by no means belonged to the most radical representatives of Reformation principles, but strove throughout to retain his connection with the Romish Church. The thirty-four articles of accusation, upon which sentence of death was passed on the former Papal

Protonotary, are partly composed of the simplest Christian axioms, embodied in quotations from the Scriptures. They nowhere express extreme views, such as those of which certain anti-Catholic Italians of that period made themselves the representatives. Were we to remember how little of unadulterated Bible truth the Papal Church can tolerate, we should then feel thankful that our Evangelical Confession has reached its present position of influence, and there is nothing more calculated to make us do so than the contemplation of the eventful fate of a man like Carnesecchi. In our statement we shall often need to let the Romish Church but speak officially, and we shall then be furnished with the keenest weapon of Protestant polemics. *Roma locuta est*, 'Rome has spoken.' She has done so here, and has spoken her own condemnation. It were idle and injurious for us to add anything thereto.

Now let us learn to know Carnesecchi more intimately.

CHAPTER II.

CARNESECCHI'S YOUTH AND EARLY LIFE AT ROME.

DANTE's native city, where scholars and artists congregated under the intellectual guidance of the Medici, was the place where Pietro Carnesecchi was born. His ancestors had long occupied an honourable position among the leading families of the Florentine Republic. Carlo Carnesecchi was one of the three distinguished citizens whose deaths the inflexible Dominican, Girolamo Savonarola, foretold, in the month of April, 1492, he being then in the vestry of St. Mark's; together with their deaths he foretold those of Lorenzo the Magnificent, of Pope Innocent VIII., and of the King of Naples.[1] One Pier Antonio Carnesecchi figures in the year 1507 as Government Commissary to the Republic, acting in the district of the Maremma; and the terms of autograph letters addressed to him by Macchiavelli, upon the part of the Florentine Council of Ten, witness the confidence which the Florentines attached to Pier Antonio's foresight and sagacity.[2]

[1] Pasquale Villari, *On Girolamo Savonarola*, translated into German by Von Berduschek. Leipzig, 1868. I.S. 111.

[2] Pasq. Villari, *On Niccolo Macchiavelli*. Florence, 1877. Vol. i., pp. 492, 617, 621.

EARLY LIFE AT ROME.

The details connected with Pietro's birth are unknown, but it must have been in the first decade of the sixteenth century that he first saw the light, for Camerarius, Melancthon's friend, in his eulogy of Carnesecchi reports, 'We know nothing definitely as to his age, nevertheless at his death, which was on the 3rd of October, 1567, he cannot have been less than 58 years of age.'

That Pietro had the advantage of a careful education, and that, living amidst the newly awakened classical studies, no branch of classical development was alien to him, is to be presumed from the importance of the Carnesecchi family, and from his own position in Florence, in addition to the evidence furnished by his posthumous letters and papers. Amongst his masters, Francisco Robertello is mentioned, who taught Greek and Greek literature in several Italian cities, his teaching of that then recently revived language having been successful; whilst it is reported that the pupil—still a youth—outstripped his master in facility of expression, both in eloquence and in composition.

Pietro as a youth was most intimate with the Medici family. The Carnesecchis attached themselves to the fortunes of the Medici, both prosperous and adverse. They did so in 1494, when the Medici were for the first time expelled; they did so in 1512, after a successful counter-revolution in Florence, which issued in their recall. The lad was Catherine's playfellow, she being of the elder branch of the family, as he also was of Cosimo, who subsequently figured in the Grand-Ducal line. Catherine and Cosimo were both born in the year 1519. No one of the three ever dreamt that Carnesecchi, the friend, would be disgracefully betrayed by Cosimo, and that Catherine would be instrumental in the instruction of posterity as to the incidents connected with Carnesecchi's fate.

Another and somewhat elder member of the Medici family who assisted Pietro, by becoming his patron, was Giuliano, the illegitimate son of Giulio, the younger brother of Lorenzo the Magnificent. He became a Churchman, and was made a Cardinal by his cousin, Pope Leo X., after whose death, in 1521, he became a candidate for Peter's chair, a position which he actually attained on the 19th November, 1523, assuming the title of Clement VII.

Pietro Carnesecchi likewise took orders whilst in Florence. In the final judgment of his process he is styled a Florentine clergyman. Whilst but a youth—we cannot accurately indicate the year—his friend Clement VII., elevated to the highest dignity in Christendom, summoned him to his Court at Rome. The most honourable reception awaited him there. Such men as Cardinal Bembo, the last representative of a period of civilization then fast fading away, the creator of the Italian grammar and the unrivalled master of Latin composition; as Cardinal Sadoleto, who combined Bembo's erudition with the piety of a really princely prelate; as the poet Marc' Antonio Flaminio; as Antonio Brucioli, the then recent translator of the Bible into Italian, who, like Carnesecchi, was by birth a Florentine; with other men distinguished by intellect and by position, at whose head was Gaspar Contarini, the Venetian, then a layman and ambassador, representing his Republic at the Papal Court, and, like the majority of those who were called 'Members of the Oratory of Divine Love,' was one of the union of clergymen and laymen, who met even in the days of Adrian VI., to promote the inward renovation and animation of the Church—all these came to meet the handsome and intelligent young Florentine, whose moral purity and exalted spirit were written upon his brow, with benevolent, friendly, and respectful feelings. Sadoleto praised him as a young man distinguished by good qualities and brilliant talents, Bembo spoke of him in terms of the highest respect and affection, and Benvenuto Cellini, the Florentine goldsmith, thanked him for his intercession, whereby he re-acquired Papal grace.[1]

[1] Goethe's Works, Vol. xxviii. Bk. ii., Cap. 2.

Clement VII. heaped proofs of his supreme good-will upon his favourite. He made him his secretary, he honoured him with the title of Papal Protonotary, he presented to him two Abbeys with all their revenues, one being in France, the other in the kingdom of Naples, at Eboli, near Salerno, and he granted to his intelligent counsellor in the many storms which he encountered during his rule over the States of the Church, many of them being directed against his own person, such widespread influence that it was commonly reported that 'the Church was more controlled by Carnesecchi than by Clement.' In his indictment it was expressly alleged against Carnesecchi, that although he was brought up at this Court of Rome, and had been most liberally endowed with dignities, ecclesiastical benefices and revenues, that nevertheless, despising the authority of the Holy Roman and Apostolic Church, he had fallen into divers heresies.

Notwithstanding his youth, and his being so manifestly favoured, he nevertheless succeeded, amidst the innumerable intrigues prompted by hatred and envy, to preserve himself uninjured and unprejudiced; nay, he, by modesty and intelligent consideration, acquired the general affection of both high and low, and this was not withdrawn from him even after the death of his patron, which occurred on the 26th September, 1534.

Whilst Clement filled the Papal Chair, Carnesecchi formed the personal acquaintance of those individuals whose mental influence subsequently gave the decisive tone to his life.

Throughout the Lent of the year 1534, there was a Capuchin monk, Fra Bernardino Ochino of Sienna, who preached the Lent sermons in Rome, in the church of San Lorenzo in Damaso. He had recently left a less austere Franciscan Order of the Observants to join this the most austere, and therefore that which, upon the part of ecclesiastical superiors, was the least approved branch of the congregation. Carnesecchi heard him preach, he learned to know him personally, and he visited him twice or thrice. The troubles which befell the Capuchin Order, and with it Ochino, just as that Order attained the sixth year of its existence, doubtless affected Carnesecchi greatly. The more lax Franciscans won over certain cardinals to their side, in order to bring about, by Papal decree, the dissolution of this new division of the Order. Drawn by this threatened danger, all the Capuchins, who then numbered but one hundred and twenty-five, were assembled at Rome. At first, by Clement's decree of April 25th, they were only expelled the city; but all the lower classes in Rome took part with them, and made demonstrations on their behalf.

Two noble women, who from the beginning of

the foundation of the Capuchin Order had joyfully hailed it as a protest against the worldliness of the cloister, combined their influence with the movement. Caterina Cibo, the Dowager Duchess of Camerino, the Pope's niece, who to her death was a warm friend of Ochino, was one of them, whilst the other was the celebrated Vittoria Colonna, the widow of Ferrante Pescara, she being at that time at Marino on a visit to her relatives, the Colonna family. These gentlewomen hurried to Rome, and so wrought upon the Pope that he withdrew his decree of expulsion. Shortly after that Clement died. Vittoria remained in Rome, and there Carnesecchi, introduced by Vittoria's friend, Cardinal Palmieri, made her acquaintance, and kissed her hand for the first time.

In 1531, at Rome, Carnesecchi learnt to know the Spanish nobleman Juán de Valdés, the spiritual founder, and subsequently the centre of the Reformation movement in South Italy, but at that time he knew him only as 'a noble knight by grace of the Emperor,' not having a notion that Valdés had 'that nobler knighthood which is by the grace of Christ.' Carnesecchi was an able statesman, and patronised classical scholarship; he was a conscientious official, and performed all the obligations of his office; a pious man, discharging as a Catholic all his ecclesiastical duties—but the decisive vital question, how man is to stand justified before God? had never as yet presented itself to him as a vital one, and hence his ear had never been roused to hear the answer, which in relation to this question had been given loudly enough in other countries.

Shortly after the death of Clement VII., Carnesecchi left Rome and wended his way home to Florence. Here he was once more brought into contact with Ochino. This was in 1536 or 1537. Ochino, the most powerful pulpit orator in Italy since the days of Savonarola, was himself, however, still entangled in Roman Catholic doctrines. He was principally indebted for his extraordinary success to the personal sincerity of his testimony, to that sympathy and love for his hearers which found expression in his sermons; whilst his absolute avoidance of scholastic disputations, which then absorbed very much of pulpit oratory, formed that element in his success which was by no means the least important.

It was Valdés' influence that first brought Ochino to the clear knowledge of the way of salvation. Ochino's testimony, however, was already a significant advance, of which many gratefully availed themselves. Assembled around his pulpit in Florence as hearers were Carnesecchi, the Duchess of Camerino, Caterina Cibo, Giberto, Bishop of Verona, Caraffa, Bishop of Chieti, afterwards Paul IV., and one who lived under the same roof as Carnesecchi—the Englishman, Reginald Pole, who had just received the Cardinal's hat, or was just about receiving it from the Pope as a recompense for his emphatic defence of the rights of the Papal throne, as opposed to the ecclesiastical caprices of Henry VIII. His nomination bears date 22nd December, 1536.

CHAPTER III.

THE INFLUENCE OF JUÁN VALDÉS AT NAPLES.

IN the summer of 1538, Carnesecchi was at the baths of Lucca, in company with Vittoria Colonna and Cardinal Pole. In 1540 he took a journey which led to his soul's turning-point. He went to Naples, probably for the purpose of being nearer to his abbey at Eboli, with a view, when necessary, to control matters there.

Juán de Valdés had several years previously settled in Naples, being a member of the Viceroy's, Don Pedro de Tolèdo's, suite, but not his secretary. Valdés must have been in every respect a distinguished personage. He was the twin brother of that Alfonso de Valdés who went with Charles V., as his Imperial Secretary, to the Diet at Augsburg; there he had varied relations with Melancthon, and translated the Augsburg Confession into Spanish for the Emperor and his Spaniards. His friend Erasmus of Rotterdam, who died in July, 1534, survived Alfonso, who died in the autumn of 1532. His brother Juán was likewise upon intimate terms with Erasmus.

Juán penetrated much deeper into the mysteries of the Holy Scriptures than did Alfonso, and especially into the Pauline doctrine of the justification of the sinner by faith. In Naples he occupied himself with philology, he studied the writings of the German Reformers, but more than them, the source of truth, the Bible itself. In it 'he lived and moved and had his being,' and in intercourse with the magnates of the Viceregal Court he managed by a quiet testimony to exert a religious influence which worked with irresistible enchantment. A contemporary styled him a missionary to the aristocracy.

That which absorbed him most was the translation and exposition of Holy Scripture. He translated the Psalms from the Hebrew, and all Paul's Epistles, with the exception of that to the Hebrews, from the Greek. Carnesecchi, however, never heard Valdés express a doubt as to who penned that Epistle; such was his testimony in one of his later examinations. Valdés wrote profound expositions upon all his translations.

His personal address, however, was most effective; his discourses, whether delivered in Naples or in the neighbouring island of Ischia—which then had been committed by King Federigo of Naples to the family of Vittoria Colonna's husband, as Governors or Castellanes—were always delivered in the presence of the most distinguished, the most pious, and the most learned inhabitants of Naples. There was the foundation laid for the practical Christian treatises of which many are only known to us by their titles.

Here the *CX. Divine Considerations* may have been written, of which the Spanish original has been lost, except thirty-nine of them, recently discovered in the Emperor Maximilian's papers in the Aulic Library at Vienna. An Italian edition of them was printed at Basle in the year 1550, and they were republished by Dr. Edward Boehmer in the year 1860.

Those who took part in these edifying conferences could, after Valdés' death, but look back upon them with regret. 'Would to God,' said Bonfadio—one who had attended them—in a letter to Carnesecchi, 'that we could once more assemble in Naples as we formerly did, although I, indeed, never dare cherish the wish, now that Valdés is dead. This has truly been a great loss to us, as it has been to all the world, for Valdés was one of the rare men of Europe, as those writings which he has left behind him testify. He was, without doubt, in his actions, in his speech, and in all his conduct a perfect man. With but a particle of his soul he governed his frail and spare body; but with the noblest part of him, with his pure understanding, as though out of the body, he was always absorbed in the contemplation of truth.'

And what names the men bore whom we find gathered around Valdés! Marc' Antonio Flaminio,

Carnesecchi's friend, the gentle-spirited poet, who spent two years at Naples for the recovery of his health, living at his villa near Caserta, who devoted himself to Valdés, as did his friends who gathered there around him. Flaminio stands a representative of the thousands in Italy who, at that time, could not resolve to break with the Papal Church, notwithstanding that they were convinced of the truth of Evangelical doctrine. There was that richly-endowed and distinguished youth, Galeazzo Caracciolo, who subsequently, for his faith's sake, severed himself from his wife and children, and fled to Switzerland, having been moved to do so by the testimonies given in this blessed circle. Aonio Paleario, who for a long time was looked upon as the author of that little book which figured in every heretical process in Italy, entitled *The Benefit of Christ*, here strengthened his faith. Peter Martyr Vermiglio, the Florentine, who from 1530 was the Abbot of the Augustines in the Monastery of St. Peter ad Aram in Naples, here learned of Valdés the right interpretation of the Pauline Epistles.

Ochino, already in 1536 in Naples, and after 1539 as General of his Order, was upon the most intimate terms with the pious Spaniard, and owed to Valdés much of the marvellous influence which he exerted in all that he did. He frequently, as Carnesecchi reports in his examination, received from Valdés, in a note written on the previous evening, the theme upon which he was to preach his sermon on the ensuing morning.

And what a bevy of noble women were they who illuminated this assembly of distinguished spirits! one of whom showed Carnesecchi the way to life eternal. We first mention Vittoria Colonna, of whom we have spoken, as having fixed her residence in Ischia, where she, about this time, passed some years, living in the castle with her sister-in-law, the Duchess of Francavilla. Still crushed under bereavement in the loss of her husband, whom she loved passionately, and whom she in her poems frequently styles 'the sun of her life,' she first found a firm stay and permanent consolation in the proclamation of mercy, of which she first heard in Valdés' circle:—

> 'Now is the Lord, who wisely has combined
> Two natures in one body, become
> My Sun and my God. I shall drink
> From the fountain, that true Helicon
> For healing all my wounds.'

Thus does she sing, and thus does she confess, in the spirit of Valdés:—

> 'Lord, wrapped in the mantle of Thy grace,
> Do I bewail my guilt, and, disburdened of all works,
> The sacred shield of faith alone protects me.'

Associated with Vittoria was Donna Isabella Brisegna; she was the sister of the Cardinal and

Supreme Inquisitor for Spain, Alfonso Manriquez de Lara. Isabella, when the storm broke forth in Italy against the Evangelicals, fled to Switzerland, and settled at Chiavenna, in the Grisons, where she lived modestly and quietly, confessing Christ, pensioned by Giulia Gonzaga with a hundred dollars a year.

From the intimations furnished in Carnesecchi's process, we learn that this tribute of love was faithfully and regularly paid by Giulia, a near relative of Vittoria's, who, like herself, was only saved by death from the persecutions of the Inquisition. Donna Giulia Gonzaga, the Duchess of Trajetto, was the widow of Vespasian Colonna, Vittoria's cousin. She was held to be the most beautiful woman in Italy, and even after retirement, in the profoundest seclusion of widowhood, and when living in the castle over her own town of Fondi, in the year 1534, the Sultan Soliman attempted to lay hands on her. His corsairs, led on by Chaireddin Barbarossa, assailed Fondi, and it was with the greatest difficulty that the terrified Duchess hurriedly escaped. Litigation with her husband's family constrained her to live at Naples, whilst her tender susceptible heart had been agonized by other painful experiences; and it was under such emotions that she first joined the Valdés' circle.

An awe-inspiring sermon of Ochino's, preached

during Lent of 1536, stripped her of her last shred of trust in her own good works and in her personal holiness—a trust which had been but a tottering one previously. On her way home from the sermon, she, having previously placed her confidence in Valdés, now poured forth to him her burdened heart; and he, like a wise lay-pastor, took this disturbed spirit in charge. He stayed with her until the night was far advanced, and directed her with all due earnestness to the Lord, to seek His grace, going on from repentance to faith. Giulia entreated him to reduce this night's conversation into writing; and we still possess it, as it appeared in Venice, in Italian, in 1546. It enables us to appreciate the soul-nursing wisdom of the man, whilst the name which he modestly assigned it was *The Christian Alphabet;* that which but teaches the elements of Christian perfection, which, when they have been appropriated, the book is to be laid aside, in order that the mind may be raised to higher considerations.

The alarm which Ochino's sermon wrought in Giulia, represents the terrors which the demands of the law impose upon the conscience. These are not to be allayed by any vows or cloistral works (Giulia was lodged in the Franciscan Convent). Faith is indispensable. Clearing this up, he added, 'When I say faith, I do not thereby mean the faith which believes in the history of

Christ; for that can, and does, exist without love; whence St. James calls it "dead faith;" for false Christians and the devils in hell possess that; but when I speak of faith, I mean that which lives in the soul, not attained by human exertion and tact, but by means of the grace of God, by supernatural light, a faith which embraces all God's Word, His threats no less than His promises; so that he, when he hears that Christ said : " He who believes and is baptized shall be saved; but that he who does not believe shall be damned;" his faith in these words, which he fully holds, inspires such confidence, that he has not the slightest doubt about his salvation.'

When Giulia thereupon replied that no man should outdo her in faith, he exhorted her to self-knowledge. 'For,' said he, 'should some one ask you whether you believe in the Creed, in every article of it, the one as much as the other, you say you do. But if, when in the act of confession you be suddenly asked whether you believe that God has forgiven you your sins, you will reply, that you think so, but that you are not sure. Now know that this uncertainty is due to want of faith. Now accept Christ's words fully which He said to the Apostles, "Whatever you shall bind on earth shall be bound in heaven, and all that you shall loose on earth shall be loosed in heaven;" and if you thoroughly believe what you confess in the Creed, when you say, " I believe in the forgiveness of sins," you will, whilst you feel pained in the soul that you should have insulted God, be able unhesitatingly to say that God has forgiven you all your sins.'

These are utterances worthy of Luther, and they penetrated Giulia's soul with vivifying power. The Duchess associated herself most thankfully with Valdés, and there was no member of his circle who understood him as she did. He dedicated his translations and expositions of the Psalms, of the Epistle to the Romans, and of the First Epistle to the Corinthians, to her.

Into this society, absorbed as it was in subjects of the most vital interest, did Carnesecchi enter, when he emigrated to Naples in the year 1540. The majority of them were already personally known to him. His friend Flaminio was the first to suggest doubts as to the truth of all the doctrines taught by the Roman Catholic Church, and Carnesecchi suggested others, whilst such doubts were, in this circle, bandied to and fro. A passage quoted from St. Augustine upon the Psalms, where it was questioned whether there was a third place besides heaven and hell, led Carnesecchi to doubt as to Purgatory; in relation to oral confession, his friend maintained that no passage could be found in the Bible which ratified its Divine institution. It was Flaminio likewise who, after he had written the last sentence of his revision, which he made in Naples, of the golden book, written by the Benedictine monk, Don Benedetto da Mantova, entitled, *The Benefit of Christ*, gave it to Carnesecchi to read, who was so delighted with it that he sent transcribed copies of it to several of his friends.

Giulia Gonzaga, Carnesecchi's high-spirited friend, assisted him to apprehend Valdés. She was the star of his life, even though Carnesecchi's innumerable letters to her, which the Inquisition afterwards laid hands on, offered his judges the most ample material whereupon to condemn him as a heretic. For years they used cypher, when mentioning either friends or enemies; thus, oo means Giulia; 55, Isabella Brisegna; 5, Carafa; 68, Valdés. Donna Giulia was ever to him a blessing from God. She helped him even during his youth, directing his future life by line and by rule, so that he avoided the rocks encountered by youth. Then she brought him to know Valdés as he without her never could have done, since he previously had known Valdés, without ever learning what that imported. Or, as he expresses himself in a letter of the 29th April, 1559: 'God has certainly employed her in order to bring me into the kingdom of God, for as soon as she had accepted Valdés' teaching she led me to adopt it.' And somewhat later: 'Donna Giulia has by her example kept me back from much that was forbidden and dishonourable, whilst she has especially delivered me from superstition and from false religion,' an observation which Carnesecchi in an examination thus interprets: 'The false religion was that which differed from the teaching and faith of Valdés, that which he had taught her and me; in that the false based salvation upon good works, whilst the latter remitted itself to faith, even as I have already so repeatedly said and declared.'

That the Neapolitan circle were conscious of a certain contradiction between official ecclesiastical teaching and their own is indubitable. They held that they could continue to be good Catholics, even when they constituted justification by faith alone the centre of their personal religious life. When the Church condemned this sentiment as heretical, and the fearful light of its vindictive rays fell upon Paul's Epistles, and amidst the willingly retained darkness of this pious community, the strong-minded ones became martyrs, the more tenderly organized and embarrassed spirits yielded and submitted themselves, as instanced in the persons of Vittoria Colonna, of Flaminio, and of so many other persons of high rank who preferred high ecclesiastical dignity to the martyr's crown.

Many admissions made by Carnesecchi at his trial show how they at Naples and elsewhere who then half unconsciously found themselves in opposition to Romish teaching, sought to put themselves right. We quote but one. Carnesecchi had written that Giulia had liberated him from the false religion. Whereupon the Inquisitors ask him, 'What, then, is religion? It is not faith alone, but all Catholic doctrine.' To which the accused replied: 'I never held it to be so. It is faith, however, which alone gives energy to religion. Had Luther and others stopped short, preaching but faith, and had they not attacked the Papacy, then would they, as Valdés and Flaminio often said to me, have been left to rank as Catholic. This doctrine of justification by faith alone embodies sentiments held by all the Fathers of the Church, by Augustine, by Chrysostom, Bernard, Origen, Hilary, Prosper, and others, and if it be not still generally received doctrine, that arises hence, that scholasticism has been more studied than the Bible.' The Inquisitors objected that the doctrine of justification by faith admitted of other heretical inferences, such as those proved by Luther, by Valdés, by the book *The Benefit of Christ*, and by that writing found amongst the accused's papers, written by Flaminio, entitled, *An Apology for the Book The Benefit of Christ*. Carnesecchi exclaimed, *Domine, vim patior, responde pro me!* 'Lord, I suffer violence, answer Thou for me.' 'Such was never my purpose. If I later went beyond

Valdés' teaching, we all nevertheless believed that the doctrine of faith was truly Catholic.' 'Why then has the accused spoken of a false religion?' 'Because we held the religion which we believed to be Catholic; and that that, on the other hand, was false, which was generally preached, especially by monks, who were much more philosophers than theologians, rather scholastic than versed in the Bible, and in the doctrine of the old Fathers. They taught, He that does what is right will go to heaven, whilst he that does that which is wrong will go to hell—and that was called Catholic, whereby they were inadvertently lapsing into Pelagianism.' 'Did he, then, believe that they who deviated from the teaching of the Catholic Church could be saved?' 'That is a question which should be addressed to a theologian, and not to me; nevertheless, I believe it, if they deviate unwittingly;' an expression which Carnesecchi thus modified at his next examination: 'I would fain rectify what I stated, it being both that which is impossible and scandalous, brought upon me by what I suffer since I am here from sleeplessness, and partly by the mere weariness and exhaustion of the examinations. I stated that they who, in matters of faith, deviate from the Holy Roman Church, doing it consciously and determinedly, are out of the way of salvation. To which, however, I ought to have added: that they who deviate from the old Church do so, whilst they that deviate from the modern one do not do so. For with relation to this modern Church, we held, that it, wanting attention and care upon the part of recent Popes, has ceased to retain that purity and sincerity of faith which existed in the Apostles.'

In this manner they pacified the mind in relation to a difference with the authorities of the Church, which they themselves could not deny. The position in relation to German and Swiss Reformers followed logically, as the result of what had been submitted. Carnesecchi was constrained to admit that a member of the Valdesian circle who had been examined before himself, Victor Soranzio, the Bishop of Bergamo, and others, had called Dr. Luther 'a great and holy father,' 'a good old man,' or 'our most distinguished teacher.' Soranzio himself was in the habit of speaking of him as *il suo buon vecchio*. When questioned, how he, Carnesecchi, judged Luther, he replied, 'We all held that Luther, so far as doctrine and eloquence were involved, was a great man; we also held that he was personally sincere in what he did; and that he only misled others when he had been misled himself by his own sentiments. We adopted some of his doctrines, whilst we repudiated others. It always displeased me that he and others had severed themselves from the

Catholic Church, partly through difference of sentiment, partly through disobedience; for he did not submit to Councils, and he opposed Popes.' Flaminio and Luigi Priuli, an intimate friend of Cardinal Pole, whom the Inquisition subsequently threatened, likewise disapproved of it, for they said: 'He who is outside of the pale of the Church is necessarily beyond charity.' ' Thus they endeavoured to pick the gold out of the dirt, and handed over what remained to the cook.'

Carnesecchi expressly and repeatedly thanked his friend Giulia, that she, by her counsels and exhortations, had preserved him from falling away into Lutheranism. But he felt more alienated from Swiss Reformers than from Lutherans. Their doctrine in reference to the Sacrament terrified him, and though opportunity did not fail him to escape to Geneva, to Zurich, or to Chiavenna, he did not avail himself of it. A letter of his upon the teaching of the Lord's Supper, written in reply to Flaminio, whose letter is dated from Trent, 1st January, 1543, is couched in very decided expressions against those who deny Christ's presence in the Sacrament : 'Where such present themselves, no confessors of, or witnesses for, the Christian faith will be found amongst them.' On the other hand, it is indeed true that he calls the Romish doctrine, an absurd and venal offering, which had long been held, to be an insult to the Lamb of God.

CHAPTER IV.

LIFE IN FLORENCE, VENICE AND PARIS.

AFTER Valdés' death, which occurred towards the close of the year 1540 or the beginning of 1541, that charming circle of Neapolitan friends was dispersed. The regulations established by the Inquisition, even as affecting Italy, by the Bull *Licet ab initio* of July 21st, 1542, soon swept away the most faithful confessors, Ochino, Peter Martyr, Galeazzo and others, out of the country; they who remained were admonished to be prudent and on their guard. It seems that Carnesecchi had, possibly before Valdés' death, or more probably in May, 1541, left Naples in company with his friend Flaminio, and with Donato Rullo, and that they went to Rome. There they lodged with the old Cardinal of Mantua *ad arcum Portugalliæ*. Rullo remained in Rome; Carnesecchi went with Flaminio to Florence, living in Carnesecchi's house from May till the middle of October. At the Capuchin Convent, three miles outside Florence, they once more saw their friend Bernardino Ochino, who had just got his sermons ready for the press, and who, but a few months subsequently, had to fly from the Inquisition.

His enthusiastic friend, Caterina Cibo, visited them in Florence, and in the autumn she accompanied them to Viterbo, where rich spiritual feasts awaited them.

Cardinal Pole had in 1539 returned to Rome, after having made several journeys on behalf of the Curia, and in the summer of 1541 he had been appointed Legate to the patrimony of St. Peter, with the residence at Viterbo. In his suite there were many adherents to the new doctrines. Luigi Priuli, the Venetian, the Abbot of San Soluto, who at the time of Carnesecchi's process was the ambassador of the Court at Savoy to the Papal Court; Fabrizio Brancuti, who subsequently fled with Piero Gelido, the Sacramentarian, to France; Apollonio Merenda, the Cardinal's chaplain, who, persecuted by the Inquisition, and subjected to torture, was condemned, and afterwards fled from Venice to Geneva, assured against further snares; Vincenzo Gherio, who, under Pius IV., was Archbishop of Ischia, Morone's adviser, and moreover that of the Pope himself, Donato Rullo, Soranzo, and others. Vittoria Colonna, in October 1541, had looked up for herself quiet quarters in Viterbo, in the cloister of St. Caterina, stating that she did so, 'because she could worship God there better and more quietly than in Rome.'

Thus when Carnesecchi and Flaminio arrived at

the Cardinal's palace, there were assembled a company of similarly minded persons, who in the intimacy of confidence weighed questions affecting man's salvation, they being all mutually interested in them. Donna Giulia sent them from Naples not only conserve of roses for the Cardinal and his friends, but also Valdés' writings, whilst the works of the Reformers circulated from hand to hand. There it was that Carnesecchi read for the first time Luther's writings, also his exposition of the gradual Psalms, and Bucer's Commentary upon the Gospel of St. Matthew. Flaminio had already given him Calvin's *Institutes* in Florence. It must have been there that Vittoria studied Luther's exposition of Psalm xlv., without being aware that the German Reformer was the author of it. Carnesecchi reports that she felt such joy and refreshment in the perusal of it, as she had never previously experienced in reading any other modern work.

Carnesecchi remained for a year in this instructive and edifying society. Confirmed in faith, enlightened in knowledge, and strengthened to testify for Christ, he left the scene of rich blessing, in company with Donato Rullo, for Venice, the city of Rullo's birth, in order to consult the medical men there in relation to an affection with which he had been tried for some time. For the first three weeks he lived under Rullo's roof.

Then he moved into his own quarters, and lived in the 'City of the Lagoons' fully three years, until 1545.

The Republic of Venice had vindicated to itself the greatest freedom and independence of any Government in Italy, as against the pretensions of Rome. Even during the Lent of 1542, though Bernardino Ochino was already held to be a heretic at Rome, and though the Roman Nuncio purposed forbidding him to preach in Venice, yet he had been appointed Lent Preacher for that year, and such was his popularity with the citizens, that the Nuncio was forced to relinquish his purpose. After the introduction of the Inquisition into Rome, the Senate of the Republic refused for a long time to raise a hand in the erection of a scaffold within its dominions; and it was not until the year 1560 that Venice carried out the first sentence of death upon matters of faith into execution. The writings of the Reformers found their way through Venice into Italy. Here Italian Bibles and other religious books were printed. The Evangelicals (the believers) of the city already, in the year 1530, warned Melancthon at the Diet at Augsburg, that he should not faint and desist from the confession of the truth; and in 1542 a letter was sent by the Churches at Venice, Vicenza, and Treviso to Luther, in which he was entreated to become the intercessor with the German Evangelical Princes for the Italian Churches, under the oppression then beginning to manifest itself.

Carnesecchi, during the three years he passed in Venice and in the cities within the Venetian territories, found numbers who sympathised with him in his religious views. The final sentence reproaches him thus :—' That has come to pass concerning thee which the Apostle says (2 Tim. iii. 13), "But evil men and seducers shall wax worse and worse, deceiving and being deceived;" for in Venice, and throughout many following years, proceeding from bad to worse, not only hast thou persisted in former heresies, but thou hast adopted others, imparting them to other persons similarly heretical and suspected, as well by reading many of the heresiarch's, Martin Luther's works, and those of other heretical and prohibited authors, as also by thy sustained intercourse with many and divers heretics.'

Amongst them the document mentions Peter Paul Vergerio, formerly the Bishop of Capo d'Istria, who just about that time was entirely won over to Evangelical views by the study of the writings of the Reformers, which he had designed to controvert; and so likewise was his brother, Giovanni Battista, Bishop of Pola. Peter Paul, after laying down his episcopal dignity in 1540, went to the Grisons, where he became a Protestant pastor. Lattanzio Ragnone, of Sienna, an enthusiastic pupil of Valdés and of Ochino, first a Lutheran, but afterwards a Zwinglian or Calvinist; and finally Baldassare Altieri of Aquila, in the Kingdom of Naples, for some time Secretary to the English Embassy at Venice, and subsequently agent there for the Protestant German Princes, and as such safely protected, the record mentions as being so many persons of his faith. The sentence stigmatizes Altieri as 'an apostate and a Lutheran, in correspondence and in harmony with the German Princes and heretical Protestants, and who assumed the monopoly of vending heretical and suspected books.' It then continues :—'And without any concern or fear, thou didst give lodging, shelter, encouragement, and money to many apostates and heretics, who, on account of heresy, fled into heretical ultramontane countries; and thou didst by letter recommend to an Italian Princess, to Giulia Gonzaga, two heretical apostates, with as much warmth as though they had been two apostles sent to preach the faith to the Turks, as thou thyself confessest, which apostates wished to open a school, with the intention of teaching their tender little scholars certain heretical catechisms; but who, as soon as they had been discovered, were forthwith sent prisoners to this Holy Office.'

It naturally came to pass that, with the ever-increasing diffusion of the new teaching, and with the severity of the measures employed to repress it, that a man like Carnesecchi could not long escape the suspicion and the proceedings of the Inquisition. Paul III., in 1546, summoned him to Rome, that he should justify himself against accusations of heresy raised against him. We cannot now ascertain the motive which induced the Pope peremptorily to drop a suit which had been instituted by the Inquisition against the Secretary and Protonotary of a predecessor in the Papal Chair. Was it an act of complacency shown to Carnesecchi's patron, Cosimo, Duke of Florence, who well knew of the Pope's desire to gain Florence? The Duke formerly wrote[1] concerning the Pope:—' He has succeeded in many of his undertakings, and now desires nothing so much as to alienate Florence from the Emperor; but he will go down into the grave with his wish unfulfilled.' Did the striking tenderness of this successor to St. Peter, shown to an aristocratic and distinguished favourer of Evangelical doctrines, illustrate Paul's then tendency to support those who had not been, up to that time, conquered by the mighty Emperor, then daily becoming more mighty? This was a tendency which Leopold von Ranke thus puts forward in his work on the *Popes of Rome*, vol. i., p. 167:—' It sounds strange, but there is nothing more true, that whilst all

[1] Ranke's *Popes*, 1874, vol. i., p. 164.

Northern Germany quaked at the prospect of the re-introduction of Papal power, the Pope felt himself to be the confederate of the Protestants.'

Let this be as it may, anyhow Paul himself intervened to protect Carnesecchi; and the exasperation which this proceeding awakened amongst the fanatical persecutors of Protestantism still rings, twenty years afterwards, in the words with which that liberation of the accused was reprehended. For Carnesecchi's judgment goes on to say :—' When a report of all these things reached the ears of Pope Paul III., of blessed memory, thou wast in the year 1546 cited to Rome, where appearing, thou wast examined by the Cardinal of Burgos, of happy memory, then an Inquisitor deputed by the Pope to be the commissary in this Holy Office of this process; and making many feigned and false excuses and replies, thou didst deny everything, and didst so palliate thy faults that thy cause was not judicially closed; but, rebuked for thy past errors and abovementioned practices, and admonished that thou shouldest in future abstain from them, from that Holy Pontiff thou didst fraudulently extort a benediction and absolution, whilst still remaining, as thou confessest, in the heresies, and under the censures and penalties thereby incurred, deluding thine own soul, and this tribunal of truth.'

That Carnesecchi, notwithstanding the Papal

pardon, no longer felt himself safe in Italy, is proved by his having left for France immediately after the trial had been stayed, in 1547, and by his stopping there no less than five years. Although, in relation to this period, he must have confessed that he had lived there soberly, and that he had concluded a truce if not a peace with sentiments adopted in Italy, and that there was an interregnum of the devil in his soul, still it must have been quite alien to a man like Carnesecchi to hold himself wholly aloof from the circles of French Protestantism. The Evangelical faith had, in spite of all the persecutions practised after Francis I.'s death (1547), under Henry II. widely extended; and there were many adherents both amongst the upper circles and the Court who protected and befriended it. Such were the two Margarets in the house of Valois; the sister of Francis I., the Queen of Navarre, and mother-in-law of Antoine de Bourbon, an enlightened Protestant; Margaret, Francis' daughter, and Henry II.'s sister, afterwards Duchess of Savoy, a quiet adherent to the new doctrine.

These at Catherine de' Medici's Court must naturally have been intimate with the well-introduced and aristocratic Florentine, drawn also the closer by sympathy in matters of faith. In his examination immediately afterwards, he maintained that in his intercourse with the Grand

Chancellor Olivier, a friend to Protestants, he had spoken much more upon scientific subjects, upon the Latin verses of Vida and of Flaminio, upon ebb and flood, upon the vacant Papal chair and the new Pope, than upon matters of faith.

Carnesecchi likewise visited the celebrated Parisian bookseller, Robert Stephens (*Etienne*), who had long been very strongly suspected of heresy at the Sorbonne. He left Paris in 1550, in order to join the Reformed faith and to settle permanently at Geneva. Carnesecchi brought him a collection of Latin hymns, written by Flaminio shortly before his death, which occurred in the year 1550. This collection Priuli had sent to Carnesecchi, 'as being rightfully his by inheritance.' The deceased poet's friend would willingly have seen the collection, which bore the title, *Upon Divine Subjects* (*De Rebus Divinis*), printed by Stephens, and then personally have placed them in the hands of the Princess Marguérite, their destination, for they had been dedicated to her by Flaminio, in this his swan-like song. But Stephens would not respond to his suggestions. Carnesecchi assumed he did not, because the book was too small and the business equally so, to admit of profit, whilst in reality the bookseller was engaged in transporting his business to Geneva. Carnesecchi then placed Flaminio's original manuscript in the

Princess's hands. This is probably the very same book of which it is said in the final judgment:— 'Out of Italy thou hadst a book sent to thee which was stained with Valdés' heresy, and didst present it as a gift.' Similarly it was there objected against him, that he, when visiting Lyons, both in going and in returning, as in Paris and at that Court, held intercourse with heretics, and that he there read Melancthon's *Common Places*, and other suspected books.

CHAPTER V.

THE ACCESSION OF PAUL IV.

UPON Carnesecchi's return journey, his friend, Lattanzio Ragnone, being in Lyons, and having in the meanwhile become pastor of the Church of fugitive Italian Protestants, sought to move Carnesecchi not to return to his unsafe Italy, but to settle down amongst them in Geneva. But Pietro withstood him, under the influence partly of the longing once more to see his friend, Donna Giulia Gonzaga, and partly of the hope that under the gentle sway of the then Pope, Julius III., who acquiesced in comfortable life too much to trouble himself about the State, the Church, and the Inquisition, he might be able to live unmolested, especially in the territory of the Republic of Venice, where he purposed again to reside. These motives caused his friend's counsel to be rejected, and he, in the year 1552, fixed his domicile at Padua, frequently alternating it with Venice.

Julius III. died March 23rd, 1555. The worthy Cardinal, Cervini, filled the Papal chair but twenty-one days, under the title of Marcellus II. After his death, which happened on Ascension Day, May 1st, the Cardinals on May

23rd, 1555, elected a man who anticipated that choice as little as did any one else, he being the most uncouth man of their number, who afterwards said, speaking of himself:—' That he never had done a kindness to any one, and that he did not know how it was that the Cardinals had fallen on him—that it must be God who made Popes.' He was Gian Pietro Caraffa, an old fellow 79 years of age, the founder and soul of the Italian Inquisition; he assumed as his own title, Paul IV., that having been the name of the Pope under whom he had been enabled to found this fearful tribunal.

Had this fanatic not been animated with one other thought of equal power—with that of liberating the Church by force from the stains of heresy —that storm would have immediately broken forth upon his elevation, which during the latter half of his reign filled the prisons of Italy and fired the faggots in which the heretics were burned. But Paul hated the Hapsburgers no less passionately. 'I will extirpate the accursed race, both father and son! Charles V. and Philip II. are heretics; they are unworthy of the earth that bears them— Charles' bedeviled soul can no longer remain in his filthy body, which, after that it is impotent, is still lecherous.' The Pope frequently indulged in such utterances as these.[1]

[1] Moritz Brosch, *Gesch. des Kirchenstaats*, 1880, p. 200.

It was fortunate for all who were not found to be immaculate in matters of faith that Paul, carried away by this passion to liberate Italy from the House of Hapsburg, occupied himself for two years perpetrating the most incredible political follies. If he throughout all that time never lost sight of his projected reform of the Church, and of the working of the Inquisition, nevertheless, the one passion of his life must necessarily have first developed itself in all its impotence, ere the other could assume despotic sway in his mind. In the mad struggle against Spain, the raving old man had to realize that that Catholic bigot, the Duke of Alba, as Philip II.'s Viceroy at Naples, marched at the head of good Catholic soldiers against Rome, whilst Paul's own troops fled before a single company of Spaniards. Christ's Vicegerent would have come to grief had not Pietro Strozzi come to the relief of the princely head of the Church by lending German Protestant warriors, who scoffed at the figures of the saints by the road-side and in the churches, who ridiculed the Mass, who made a joke of fasting, and who did a hundred things any one of which, at another time, he would have visited with death.[1]

After the disgraceful peace of Cavi, concluded on September 14th, 1557, with which the Pope

[1] Von Ranke's *Roman Popes*, vol. i., p. 190.

terminated the political dream of his inglorious life; after having laid waste half Italy, the irritated and thwarted old man spent his rage upon heresy, which still raised its head all over the peninsula. Already in the summer the prisons of the Inquisition were full. On June 5th, 1557, Carnesecchi, being in Venice, wrote to Giulia Gonzaga, that together with San Felice, Bishop of La Cava, one of the most distinguished of all the Cardinals had had to go into the Castle of St. Angelo as a prisoner; Giovanni Morone, the son of Girolamo Morone, the Milanese Chancellor, who had been so deeply involved in an intrigue with Vittoria Colonna's gallant husband, Pescara.

Carnesecchi stood in relation to Morone in the position of a most intimate adherent and friend. Their fathers had mutually honoured and loved each other. Pietro called Giovanni Morone (born in 1509) his earliest master and patron, into whose service he had entered in 1527, before he became Bishop of Modena. When Clement VII., in 1535, made Morone Bishop of Modena, he dispensed him from the canonical altar, on account of his rare virtues. That Morone, in spite of his many embassies to Germany in the service of the Papal chair, believed in justification by faith after the view of Valdés, and that he was guilty of sympathy with the Evangelicals, is not to be denied. Nevertheless, his imprisonment made men shudder. Carnesecchi wrote to Giulia in Naples on June 12th, 1557, 'Why Morone is imprisoned, no one knows; many say that the Cardinals have brought it about, in order that he may be out of their way at the next election of a Pope, when he would get the greatest number of votes. The Pope intends summoning all the Cardinals to Rome, that they as a College may judge Morone. Paul IV. has also summoned Soranzio of Bergamo, and Foscarari, Bishop of Modena, and a Dominican monk, to Rome. Now that temporal war has been brought to a close, it appears that a spiritual one shall commence, in order that the world be not idle, but shall ever have opportunity to exercise both spirit and flesh.'

Besides those above named, there were many other Church dignitaries arrested and proceeded against; the Abbot Villamarino, Morone's house steward; a Venetian, called Bishop Centanni, Don Bartholomeo Spatafora; the Archbishop Mario Galeota of Sorrento, the Bishop Verdura, and others. Cardinal Pole, too, who sought, at the Court of Bloody Mary, first as Cardinal-Legate and then as Archbishop of Canterbury, in the exercise of a wise moderation, to bring England back to her dependence on the Papal See, did not escape Paul IV.'s keen sense of suspicion. By a Brief, dated August 9th, he was cited to

Rome to purge himself from suspicion of heresy. Violent intermittent fever, and the Queen's resistance, who would not allow her friend to be dragged away, fortunately for him, retained him in England till his death, which took place on November 18th, 1558, sixteen hours after that of the Queen, and delivered him from all the dangers that Paul IV. had devised, notwithstanding all Pole's devotion to the Papal See, which was such as to be scandalous to his former friends, for Pole's last years could not but be offensive to his old associates at Naples and Viterbo.

Carnesecchi wrote to Donna Giulia :[1] 'Would that Pole had died when he came forth so gloriously out of Pope Julius' conclave. For at his death he was held at Rome to have been a Lutheran, in Germany a Papist, at the Court of Flanders a Frenchman, and at the French Court an Imperialist.' Shortly before his death Pole made a declaration that he firmly held the Catholic faith, and that he held the Pope, and not, indeed, excluding the one then in the chair, to be really the vicar of Christ and Peter's successor. Carnesecchi, moreover, taking up an expression of Giulia's, stated that in a letter to her which afterwards weighed heavily upon him. He wrote on February 11th, 1559: 'It has gratified me extraordinarily that Donna Giulia disapproves Pole's

[1] Page 130 of MS.

declaration, for it practically is superfluous, if not offensive, and especially so at the present time.'

Although Carnesecchi thought of it just as did Donna Giulia, still, from diffidence, he would say nothing. 'Nevertheless, there is a great difference between Pole and Valdés, and with both is that verse verified :

"As evening characterises the day, so does death life."

Well, then, we will thank God that our faith does not depend on men, neither are its foundations laid on sand, but on the everlasting rock, upon which the Apostles and Prophets, and all God's saints have similarly built theirs. May God be pleased to grant us grace to live and to die steadfastly therein!'

CHAPTER VI.

THE PERSECUTION UNDER PAUL IV.

In the meanwhile, Carnesecchi, too, found himself brought into unpleasant personal contact with the Inquisition. Paul IV. on his part could not allow the man who so unexpectedly had escaped him to pass unassailed. He cited him by a Decree of October 25th, 1557, to appear before a General Assembly of 'the Holy Cardinals of the Inquisition' at their tribunal at Rome, there personally to clear himself from the accusation of having long adhered to many Lutheran articles, of having had heretical books, and of having maintained intercourse with heretics. The citation was personally served on him at Venice, on November 6th.

Carnesecchi refused to appear at Rome, and was bold enough to remain at Venice. The Republic had just withstood inducements held out to it by Paul to enter into a confederation against the Spaniards, as also against his extensive promises that the Island Queen should hold Sicily for evermore as her own. These propositions she obstinately rejected, for she met them with deep distrust—hence there arose, as frequently happened, strained relations between Venice and Rome.

Carnesecchi, in his reliance thereupon, dared to defy the Pope and his citation. The consequence was that the accused was declared, by a decree issued by the Inquisition, dated March 24th, 1558, having the expressed assent of the doctors, theologians, and canonists, to have incurred the censures and penalties threatened in the citation; and this declaration was published contemporaneously in Rome and in Venice.

As this step likewise achieved nothing, final judgment was delivered on April 6th, 1559, whereby Carnesecchi was declared to be a heretic in contumacy, and he was sentenced to the punishments which attach to impenitent heretics. All his property, movable and immovable, was confiscated; he was deprived of his benefices, and the warrant issued against him notified that he, when seized, would be handed over to the secular arm.

It may be imagined that Carnesecchi, in spite of the protection which he anticipated in Venice, must nevertheless have lived an oppressive and anxious life during these years. Describing it, he says that he felt like a wild beast, in continuous fear and anxiety amidst the hostility which surrounded him. The zeal of the decrepit old Pope waxed with every additional person cast into the dungeons of the Inquisition, as also at the escape of every one who evaded them. Distinguished Church dignitaries in the cells of Roman prisons were daily threatened with the rack; even Cardinal Morone was, according to a letter of Donna Giulia, exposed to torture. Paul IV. was so enraged at Pole's death, that he declared that he would by every possible means reveal what a heretic and rebel he had been. Carnesecchi, writing upon this subject to Donna Giulia, said, 'Whereby the Pope will assuredly more reveal his own folly and iniquity, than obscure the memory and the fame which so excellent a man had bequeathed to all, and especially to good men.'

The Duchess of Trajetto, Vittoria Colonna, did not dare to leave Naples, because she feared lest she should fall into the Pope's hands as one suspected of Valdésian heresy. The Duke Cosimo of Florence interceded for Carnesecchi, but in vain. The Pope requested the Venetian Senate to deliver up the condemned one; the first time unsuccessfully. But Carnesecchi doubted whether a second application would not issue in his being banished from their territory. The refugees in Switzerland likewise often sought to move him to spontaneous flight. The Count Galeazzo Caracciolo entreated him to flee, when he, in the summer of 1558, having a safe-conduct from the Viceroy, to visit his family left behind by him in the kingdom of Naples, went there in order to move them to share his exile—an effort in which he was vigorously supported by Carnesecchi.

Freedom to be able to live after a man's heartfelt religious convictions; the Gospel preached in all its purity in the countries to which the Reformation had extended; the zeal with which the Holy Scriptures was read and expounded; the more frequent administration of the Lord's Supper; the temptation to insult God by daily recurring idolatry and other reckless acts performed by the man who irresolutely limps when seeking to follow both sides—all this powerfully attracted Carnesecchi to the reformed Swiss Cantons, besides his being at all times threatened with personal danger.

But, on the other hand, there was much to retain him in alienation from the doctrines held by Zwingle and by Calvin on the Sacrament; his heart's yearning to remain as near as possible to his friend Giulia, in the hope of resuming his intimacy with her; the hesitancy lest he, by his flight, should possibly injure his patrons and friends who were in the prisons of the Inquisition in Rome. Then again, he, like many others, hoped that a new Pope might, from Paul's great age, ere long present himself, the strings of whose administration would not be strung up so taut.

On March 25th, 1559, and hence on the day after his definitive condemnation in Rome, where, as he thought, his effigy would have been publicly burnt by the Inquisition, Carnesecchi writes to Giulia: 'When I think on the good grounds which

Carnesecchi has to calculate on the favour and help which present themselves in different directions to him, as also on the goodwill and amiability which Popes are wont to manifest when they begin their rule, I do not for a moment doubt but that he will be rehabilitated and honourably reinstated—unless a Bull have been issued against him, which the Pope shall have launched against persons in the same predicament as his. In the meanwhile this has not been published, and will, on the other hand, from what I hear, be so unjust that it is to be hoped that his successor will not carry it out—unless he should prove to be an Alessandrino;' (by whom he meant Cardinal Michele Ghislieri, Paul IV.'s Commissary General of the Inquisition, who in 1566 actually became Pope, styling himself Pius V.)—'from him or any one like him, may God preserve us!'

The tough, wiry frame of the old monk filling the Papal chair still resisted death. Carnesecchi felt perplexed as to what he ought to do. The Cardinal of Trent, kindly disposed to him, advised that he should write to the Pope, apparently submitting himself to him, and stating that he was too unwell to ride on horseback; and that this would help him, if not with the present Pope, at least with his successor. Carnesecchi thought of migrating to his native Tuscany, where he anticipated assured protection by Cosimo, or to

France, or to England. But the news of Caraffa's death came at last.

With what a shout of joy this was hailed throughout the earth! Whilst the Pope was still struggling with the agony of death, the Romans already rose in revolt. This was on August 18th, 1559. 'In the Capitol a decree was formulated by which the prisons were to be opened; then the wild masses spread themselves throughout the city. They first stormed the building of the Inquisition, they threw all its documents out of the windows, and they plundered Cardinal Ghislieri's apartments, he being the highest resident authority; they did the same to the other officials, personally maltreating them; they set fire to and burned part of the palace down. The news of the Pope's death having spread, they hurried to Santa Maria sopra Minerva, they liberated those who were incarcerated there, and would have burnt down that convent, and have thrown the monks out of the windows, had they not been prevented by Giuliano Cesarini. The other prisons, the Torre Savella, the Tor di Nona, and that of the Senators, were also broken open; they set at liberty four hundred prisoners, of whom but seventy had been placed in charge by the Inquisition, however, of them forty-two were arch-heretics. But they went on worse the day after Paul's death. Some months previously, when Paul's two nephews fell, a statue had been erected to the Pope in the Capitol. This statue now became the object upon which the people vented their fury. The magistracy assembled very early. The open space was soon thronged. The populace pulled the statue down from its pedestal, and broke it up; whilst the magistracy and the higher orders looked on and laughed when they saw a Jew put his yellow cap upon the Pope's head. Throughout that live-long day did this head remain as the butt for the contempt of the rabble, but towards evening some persons, moved by commiseration, threw it into the Tiber. And when the festivities attained their height upon the third day, the Sunday, all the inscriptions and arms of the Caraffa were smashed and obliterated.' Such is the report of a decidedly Catholic historian.[1]

Can any one blame Carnesecchi if he experienced joy at this death? Nevertheless he was blamed for doing so. In as late an examination as that of December 14th, 1566, the Inquisitors put this interrogatory to him—Why had he so earnestly desired the Pope's death? and when consummated, why had he so greatly rejoiced? This was his noble reply—' I do not think that such a question needs to be answered; the thing

---

[1] Alfred von Reumont, in his *History of the City of Rome*, vol. iii., part 2, pp. 542, 543.

speaks for itself.' The Cardinals proceeded—Had he rejoiced at the fire which burnt the palace of the Inquisition, situate in the Ripetta, in connection with the death of Paul IV. of happy memory? 'Certainly, I cannot conscientiously deny it; because I hoped in relation to myself and to others that my process would be dispatched by this fire, and that theirs would be facilitated.' Asked whether he attributed this fire to the judgment of God, visited because of the persecution of heretics? Neither would he deny this; for if indeed he had never said or written it, he assuredly had thought it. Whether he had rejoiced over the liberation of those who were being examined by the Inquisition in that palace? Indeed he had. Why did he hold them to be innocent? Because he thought that they had but retained the article of justification by faith.

Carnesecchi fortunately answered all these questions correctly—for frequently he never surmised with what purpose the questions were put to him—as, for instance, whether he had ever wished that Paul should meet an early death, &c., &c. These questions were based upon statements made by Carnesecchi in his correspondence, but which he had long forgotten. The following reflections by the accused, made in a letter to Donna Giulia, on September 2nd, 1559, were adduced against him as evidence:—' Your ladyship will have heard that the Holy Inquisition has died the same death by which she was wont to put others to death, that is by fire. And certainly this is a very remarkable event, from which the conclusion may be drawn, that it cannot be acceptable to the Divine clemency that this Office henceforth proceed with the same strictness and severity as it has in the past. It ought rather to deal amiably, as exemplified by former Popes—a line of conduct which is much more becoming.'

CHAPTER VII.

REVERSAL OF THE FIRST SENTENCE AGAINST CARNESECCHI.

CARNESECCHI, believing in the merits of his cause, now went to Rome to get his process reviewed. The Duke Cosimo had promised him that he would, were it needed, put horses and cavaliers in motion to support him, and to assist him to attain his rights. Morone for a long period had the greatest prospect of ascending the Papal throne; but he, when Paul IV. closed his eyes, was a prisoner in the Castle of St. Angelo. The College of Cardinals determined—Carnesecchi states it in writing—that his process was null and void, false and iniquitous; and as such, deserving to be burnt; and the burning was actually carried out before them all. Cosimo, too, at Florence, supported Morone's nomination with unusual earnestness. Carnesecchi's letters of this period speak out respecting the Papal election with great openness. 'Should Morone become Pope,' says he, on October 18th, 1559, 'we could wish him to lay aside one fault which he showed when he voted for Paul IV., viz., his faint-heartedness.'

The Cardinal Medici, who was nominated at

the same time as Morone as the future Pope, and who was actually elected by the Conclave, had given the promise—Carnesecchi vouches it— that were he appointed Pope, he would give the German clergy permission to marry, and the Communion in both kinds, if they would come back to the other teaching of the Church. 'Even Aracœli has hopes,' (so says Carnesecchi in a letter to Giulia, written when travelling from Florence to Rome, on December 2nd, 1559), 'although he is a monk, which is looked upon as a second original sin added on to that which man ordinarily has.'

Giovanni Angelo Medici, a Milanese upstart, insignificant by birth, but an amiable, kindly-disposed man, was elected Pope on December 25th, as Pius IV. On January 3rd, 1560, Carnesecchi wrote from Pisa:—'I start for Rome the day after to-morrow, where I hope that my matter will issue well, not only because of its inherent goodness and rectitude, which cause it to be commended to His Holiness, but because of the authority and of the favour which my Prince has in his sight.'

But, in the meanwhile, things did not move forward so smoothly as he had hoped. Carnesecchi, by the advice of his patrons, lived in great retirement. He only went out at night, or if by day, in a carriage. Morone exercised great influence upon Pius IV. in his decisions; but Morone at first did not dare to open his mouth on behalf of his friend, 'and acted as though apparently he did not know him. His others patrons also interposed on his behalf rather by consolatory promises than by practical assistance. The revision of his process dragged its weary way from week to week and from month to month. In spite of the favour that Carnesecchi enjoyed amongst those who surrounded the Pope, he had to remain in a sort of imprisonment in the Cloister of the Servites, St. Marcellus, on the Corso. He was not confined within its walls, but he only went out at night, and then with the modesty and quietness that had been imposed upon him.

He wrote on August 31st that he no longer looked for his liberation from men, nor from the Pope, but from God only. The Cardinal of Trent, who had been appointed an Inquisitor, visited him in his convent in September, and in October Cardinal Seripando, who likewise was one of his friends, and who had been nominated one of the Holy College, came to him. At length the Duke Cosimo made his appearance in Rome, and sought personally to move the Pope on his behalf. But his destiny was again controlled by his evil star. The Duke fell sick, and the Duchess, who also had promised Carnesecchi to help him, could do nothing, for she was wholly absorbed in nursing. At last Pius declared that he would judge this matter himself, partly because he had Carnesecchi's honour at heart, and partly out of consideration for the Duke and Duchess. Then, 'changeable as a leaf,' he withdrew his promise, and said that he would see to it that no injustice should be done to Carnesecchi.

Under date of December 5th, 1560, Pietro writes in despair:—' Nothing progresses! The fault lies with the Inquisitors, partly because they will not judge as right and duty dictate, for they suggest scrupulous hesitancy where there is no ground for it, and interpret that prejudicially which, rightly apprehended, is good and praiseworthy. O God, pardon them who sin through ignorance ; but the others so convert or ruin, that they may be unable daily to injure the innocent! As to Seripando, there is no placing reliance on him, for he does not take his seat at the tribunal ; he is sick, and would willingly act the truant, for he well knows the difficulties, and wants the courage to encounter them single-handed.'

Later on the Pope permitted Carnesecchi himself to visit the Duke, and to plead his own cause, but only in Ghislieri's presence. 'I never feared but that my innocence would make itself manifest, even had there been seven Alessandrinis instead of one.' On December 13th, Carnesecchi was admitted to the Pope's presence, for the Pope determined to withdraw the process from the tribunal, and to deliver judgment thereupon himself. But this was unsatisfactory to Carnesecchi, who feared that benevolence exaggerated would but lead to protracted proceedings. In a letter on January 23rd, 1561, he says :—"I have had so much to do, in reflecting upon the answers, and how to formulate them which I have to give to my—shall I call them judges or opponents?—that I have scarcely found time to eat and to sleep, less time to write about my affairs, which, after all, encountered such a storm that I at times was constrained to fear shipwreck. But now it is all right, and I am so near the haven that I can say I am in safety. My storms sprang from my refusal to deny the favourable opinions which I hold of Valdés and of Galeazzo Caracciolo, in doing which I necessarily vindicated certain propositions of Valdés, by which the judges were the more exasperated. But since I have cleared myself, they must digest their choler.'

Finally, on May 8th, 1561, after a year and a-half's anxiety and privation, he was able to write :—'All has been considered, deliberated upon and ventilated by these my illustrious and most reverend Lords Cardinals, and has issued well, as the tenor of the subjoined sentence proves, which, dictated and composed by my own advocate, concurs fully and entirely with what I could have wished. I beg you to send it on to Monsignor Mario (Galeota, the Archbishop of Sorrento), in order that he may see that I too am an Israelite, and that he henceforth will not have so much to fear in responding to my salutations, since he himself may now rejoice over my liberation.'

Carnesecchi appears to have remained in Rome until October. Then he went to Naples, to salute his friends, who had taken such heartfelt interest in his fate. He lodged with the monks of San Giovanni in Carbonaria, whom the Cardinal Seripando had to order over and over again to give Carnesecchi his own room; it was only with suppressed rage that the monks received the suspected person. He afterwards must have travelled about a great deal. In his final judgment he was reproached that after his liberation he still occupied himself with heretics and heresy, in Rome, in Naples, in Florence, in Venice, and in other parts of Italy, upholding suspected persons with counsel and with funds. The last letter cited in extracts in the proceedings was one addressed to Donna Giulia of November 24th, 1563, from the Abbey of Casal Nuovo (she died in 1566). He says, 'Be not surprised at my great activity or wantonness, when you contemplate me rushing, like Cæsar, with such rapidity throughout all Italy. I feel more robust than ever. It appears to be God's will to compensate me here on earth for the sicknesses and other afflictions which, sent me by Him, I have patiently borne.

God, too, has given me this abbey, after that He had taken the other, Eboli, from me.'

Surely everyone will understand that this, Carnesecchi's second liberation from the toils of the Inquisition, would be borne with the greatest exasperation both by it and its friends. The mode in which this act of the Pope was judged in these circles finds expression, notwithstanding all prudence and reverence, in Carnesecchi's final judgment. There it states, in relation to this last depicted period :—' After Paul IV.'s death, thou hast by various ways and means endeavoured with many artifices and importunate entreaties, and with certain feigned excuses, made to Pope Pius IV., of happy memory, that thou shouldest be admitted to an audience, which thou couldest not have been admitted to, had it not been for his clemency, since thou hadst been legally condemned as a convicted heretic. And to excuse thy faults, which thou hast dissimulated and concealed, according to thy habit, at thy examinations of that period, partly by feigning ignorance, and partly by not only not revealing thine errors against the holy faith, but likewise by not satisfying general interrogatories upon the subjects upon which thou wast inquisited, it appearing to thee that thou wert not under obligation to reveal them. And then in the special interrogatories by equivocating and avoiding to answer them simply, and partly by taking counsel with the talent of thy prison, thou hast had certain answers and declarations put in thy mouth, both by some others who had been inquisited for heresy, but who had been set at liberty, and by certain theologians, making every effort, by fraudulent persuasions and illicit modes, in order that thou mightest be set free as being innocent, and absolved by the Holy Office from the imputations alleged against thee, which thou oughtest, for thy salvation, sincerely to confess, and publicly to abjure and detest, in order to be admitted by grace into the bosom of the Church. Which thou hast done out of regard to worldly honour, and to avoid the punishments due to heretics, causing many witnesses to be examined to confirm thy falsehoods, and in order, as thou saidst, to canonize thee, and for the justification of thy masters and companions. Whence by thy artifices and false pretences, and through certain writings and proceedings having been burnt in the fire of the Ripetta, by which the truth might have been cleared up, thou didst so far succeed that, instead of a severe condemnation, thou hast extorted, and that iniquitously, a sentence of absolution, as though thou hadst always been an innocent and good Catholic; and, nevertheless, thou hast under thine own hand declared and confessed that all the accusations made against thee were most true, and that thy excuses and justifications were simulated and feigned, as well those of the process made in the days of Pius as in those of Paul, and to the greater damnation of thy soul; and, deceiving His Holiness the first-named Pope, thou hast obtained from him, surreptitiously and clandestinely, a *motu propio* confirmatory of the above sentence.'

That such a head of game should have escaped it was constantly present to the mind of the Holy Office. It was on the watch for a more favourable opportunity to spend its wrath upon the man who had twice got out of its meshes. And this opportunity presented itself.

In spite of all the warnings from abroad, from those friends of Carnesecchi who had fled and lived there in safety, he could not make up his mind to leave his native land. In 1565 he was again in Venice, where he was the year prior to that in which Giulia died, he having induced her, in 1564, to send to him at Venice the writings of Valdés which she had, lest possession of them should imperil her. In the meanwhile Carnesecchi's ruin was rapidly hastening on.

CHAPTER VIII.

THE FINAL TRIAL, ARTICLES OF CONDEMNATION AND MARTYRDOM OF CARNESECCHI.

PIUS IV., the gentle Pope, died early in December, 1565. The Pope elected by the Conclave was Paul IV.'s supreme Inquisitor, the ferocious and inexorable Dominican, Michael Ghislieri, the Cardinal of Alessandria, who assumed the title of Pope Pius V. Under his control, which with keen and persistent energy insinuated itself whereever opportunity offered, clemency became a thing of the past, and 'one Alessandrino,' occupying the Papal chair, was perfectly able to ruin Carnesecchi.

We have witnessed with what repeated welcomes Duke Cosimo of Florence had received the friend of his house. It was with him that Carnesecchi sought protection when his most bitter enemy attained the supreme rule of the Church. But how did Ghislieri's reckless energy paralyse others! Cosimo, too, was destined to feel its influence.

Carnesecchi was a guest at his sovereign's table when the friar Tomaso Manrique, the Master of the Papal Palace, was announced, as sent on a special mission to Florence, and desiring an interview with the Duke. The Pope had furnished his messenger with a letter bearing date June 20th, 1566, in which, after greeting Cosimo with the Apostolic Benediction, 'he was called upon, in an affair which nearly affected obedience to the Divine Majesty and to the Catholic Church, and which the Pope had greatly at heart, as being of the highest importance, to give to the bearer of this letter the same faith as though His Holiness were present conversing with him.' Manrique claimed in the Pope's name the delivering over of Carnesecchi into the hands of the Inquisition. The Duke made his friend and guest rise from the table and surrender himself on the spot to the Papal messenger. And he abjectly added, that, 'had His Holiness—which God forefend—called upon him to surrender his own son for the same motive, he would not have hesitated one moment to have him bound and surrendered.'

Carnesecchi found opportunity before his incarceration in Florence to give orders to his household to get all his suspected books, by Luther, by Peter Martyr, by Calvin, together with Flaminio's Apology for *The Benefit of Christ*, out of the way. Whilst being transported to Rome, he wrote that they should be thrown into a well. It seems that the only suspected books found were the Apology and a manuscript in quarto of twenty-four sheets, which had been dedicated to the Duchess

Giulia Gonzaga, entitled, *Meditations and Prayers upon St. Paul's Epistle to the Romans.* Carnesecchi at his examination of March 7th, 1567, declared it to be a work of Marcantonio Flaminio. It is also possible that the extraordinarily voluminous correspondence of Carnesecchi with the Duchess may after her death have been returned to him by her relatives, and have subsequently been found in his dwelling by the Inquisition. Anyhow, these letters furnished the leading evidence which the tribunal of the Inquisition availed itself of to his condemnation.

'The Master of the Sacred Apostolic Palace' led his prisoner to Rome, where he was lodged in the prison of the Holy Office. The first examination was held on July 13th, 1566,[1] upon which there followed an interminable series of hearings, in the highest degree fatiguing and galling. Moreover, the rack was employed upon Carnesecchi; and his judges made it a subject of special reproach that he, under torture—*sotto l'esamine rigoroso*—remained obstinate, and expressed himself unintelligibly.

The Duke of Florence, who now earnestly exerted himself upon behalf of the man whom he had so basely surrendered, received as reply to his intercession for mercy, that the Pope, since the prisoner was in the hands of the Inquisition, could

[1] There were other examinations prior to that of July 13th. Manzoni, in his preface to the *Estratto*, alludes to them.

no longer do anything himself for him. Carnesecchi wrote from his dungeon to Morone, to the Cardinal of Trent, to the Abbot of San Soluto, to Bartholomeo Concino, that he was being tortured ; that his judges held him to be insincere : 'They would fain have me say of the living and of the dead things which I do not know, and which they would so fain hear.' These letters were seized, and served with the judges of that tribunal but to enhance Carnesecchi's guilt.

These investigations were carried on through fifteen months' imprisonment. Sentence was delivered by the tribunal of the Inquisition on August 16th, 1567, and was published to the world on September 21st, in Santa Maria sopra Minerva, when the prisoner was handed over to *the secular arm*,' and was then led away to the most terrible prison in Rome, to the Tor di Nona, situate near the Ponte St. Angelo, where isolated cells were rendered pestilential and disgusting by having putrid water in them, from which he was only to be delivered by death, inflicted with the infamy of a public execution.

But the articles of faith, the acceptance of which Rome declared to be a crime worthy of death, deserve to be published throughout the world. A Church which visits such things with death at the stake has not condemned the heretic, but it has condemned itself. Carnesecchi was found guilty upon thirty-four points of accusation; and our readers may insist that no one of them be withheld from their knowledge. The version given here coincides with that found in Manzoni's *Estratto*, in Italian, and with that given by Schelhorn, in Latin.

'That thou, from the year 1540, and in succeeding years, hast held and believed the following propositions, which are severally heretical, erroneous, rash, and scandalous :—

'1. Justification by faith alone, and that our works have no part in it; according to Luther's, the heresiarch's, teaching, in connection with the Epistle to the Galatians.

'2. The certainty of grace and of salvation, according to the same Luther.

'3. That our works are not essential to salvation, which is to be obtained through faith; but that the justified man would inevitably perform them whenever he should find time and opportunity.

'4. And, consequently, that the said good works could not merit everlasting life; but would indeed be rewarded with a higher degree of glory after the general resurrection.

'5. Thou hast held concerning Fasts, that it is not a mortal sin not to observe them, unless this omission should arise from contempt; but that they are useful for mortification only.

'6. That we have by nature a free will to do evil; and, before grace, only to commit sin.

'7. That it is not possible to keep the commandments in the Decalogue, and especially the first two, and the last, "Thou shalt not lust after," without the most effectual influence of the grace of God, and without a great abundance of faith and of the Spirit, which is found but in few; and the case is not so with every ordinary Christian, but with the perfect, such as the holy Martyrs and Doctors of the Church have been.

'8. That we ought not to believe anything save that which is the word of God expressed in Holy Scripture.

'9. That not all General Councils are assembled in the Holy Ghost, and therefore that we should not have faith in the decisions of them all; exercising a critical judgment as to which may be those assembled in the Holy Ghost; and questioning whether the power to convoke them belonged to the Emperor or to the Pope, or to others.

'10. Thou hast been undecided respecting the number of the Sacraments, having heard that Calvin held two, namely, Baptism and the "Supper" (as thou art wont sometimes to call the most Holy Eucharist); and that Luther added to them Orders, which thou termest "the Imposition of Hands."

'11. Thou hast in like manner been uncertain as to whether the Sacrament of Confirmation was instituted by Christ or by the Church, holding that it was the ratification of the promises made in Baptism.

'12. That Sacramental Confession was not established by Divine command, nor appointed by Christ; and that it cannot be proved by Scripture; and that none was indispensable except that which is made to God; and therefore that it was left at the option of a Christian to go, or not to go, to confess; although it might be beneficial and consolatory to the penitent, as to the comfort which he might derive from absolution, and as to the advice and the remedies which he might receive; and such was thy opinion up to the time when thou didst acknowledge thy delinquency before this tribunal.

'13. Thou hast held that the satisfaction which consists of penitential works, imposed by priests upon those who are contrite, was not necessary (upon the presumption that it took the place of the merit of Christ, as sufficient to atone for the sins of the whole world); but that such works were good for the purposes of mortifying the flesh, and giving life to the spirit.

'14. That Indulgences were not founded on Holy Scripture, but were invented by the Popes ; and were not available except for the living, as to the penances imposed on them by the Pope, or by other priests.

'15. Thou hast maintained the uncertainty of Purgatory, concerning which thou hast entertained strong doubts, or rather hast actually held, that it has no real existence after the present life ; but that the blood of Christ was the purgatory for our sins—not having become convinced by the places of Holy Scripture which are cited in support of this truth, up to the period of thy aforesaid confession.

'16. Thou hast considered as apocryphal the Book of the Maccabees, in which mention is made of prayers for the dead.

'17. That in the most holy Sacrament of the Eucharist the substance of bread remained, while there was also in it the presence of the Body of Christ, without Transubstantiation having taken place, according to the opinion of Luther, to which thou hast adhered since the year 1543 ; although sometimes thou wast pleased with, and favourable to, the heresy of Calvin ; to which also thou gavest attention, and discussing which with others, thou hast reasoned as well as written.

'18. Thou hast held and believed that it was better that the laity should communicate in both kinds than in one.

'19. That the most holy Sacrifice of the Mass was not truly propitiatory, except so far as it excites in us the remembrance of the passion of Christ, and consequently that faith by which the forgiveness of sins is obtained.

'20. That the Pope possessed supremacy over other Bishops, not in the way of jurisdiction, but simply by pre-eminence ; and this thou hast for some time believed.

'21. And thus that the Pope was only Bishop of Rome, and that he had no ascendency over other Churches, beyond what might be conceded by the world, from respect to the See of Peter ; as also on account of the dignity and greatness of

Rome; and because that city had been ennobled by the blood of so many thousands of martyrs.

'22. That the Roman Pontiffs had unjustly claimed for themselves, in sundry matters, more authority than they had received from God; and especially with regard to Indulgences and predominance over other Churches.

'23. And thou hast for a certain period suspected that the succession of the Roman Pontiffs terminated with the Apostleship of St. Peter.

'24. Thou hast blamed several Orders and Rules of Monks and Friars (as those of St. Benedict, and others), for leading an idle and useless life, and for being persons who had as it were been "born to consume the fruits of the earth;" and thou foundest fault with some fraternities of Mendicants also, and their bags; saying such things as that, "they took the bread out of the hand of the poor;" and that "they would do better to work with their own hands, and live by the sweat of their brows."

'25. And although thou hast approved of the zeal of those monks who labour hard in the vineyard of the Lord, preaching and watching over the salvation of their neighbours, thou hast, nevertheless, held that their zeal was not "according to knowledge;" as it appeared to thee that works were put forward too prominently in their preaching.

'26. With respect to celibacy, thou hast conceived that it would be better to restore wives to priests than to have deprived them of them.

'27. That to the vow of single life members of the Religious Orders could not, and should not, bind themselves; and that it would be inexpedient for them to do so; chastity and continence being gifts of God; and on this account that they cannot be promised, except by those who by long experience have been enabled to ascertain that they have received such a faculty from Him; and for this reason thou didst advise and encourage a Benedictine monk (equally heretical, and thy accomplice), who was disposed to desert his Order, to leave it.

'28. And thou hast had the same opinion relative to Nuns and Virgins who devote themselves to God; and such has also been thy judgment with regard to the mere vow of permanent continence.

'29. Thou hast questioned whether Pilgrimages and visits to churches, undertaken spontaneously, or in consequence of vows, are suitable for all kinds of persons; nay, rather thou hast said that these vows respecting Pilgrimage are worthless to every one without exception.

'30. That all sorts of food, without any choice, may be eaten, according to the conscience of him who partakes of them, and thou hast acted upon this supposition.

'31. And that it would not be a mortal sin to disregard the observance of days and seasons of restraint by making use of forbidden kinds of food; but that it would be a greater or less offence in proportion to the scandal thereby occasioned, and according to the accusing or excusing of one's own conscience.

'32. That it is not a sin to keep or to read heretical or prohibited books; but a matter of indifference, and one to be decided by the conscience of him who possesses them, notwithstanding the interdict of the Holy Church.

'33. From the year 1543 until 1545, and from 1557 till 1559, thou hast held that, Christ being the only Mediator between God and men, it was unnecessary to pray to the saints; and for some time thou hast not done so.

'34. And, lastly, thou hast believed all the errors and heresies comprised in the said book *Of the Benefit of Christ*, as well as the false doctrine and principles taught by the said JUÁN VALDÉS, thy master.'

These were the articles of faith, for holding of which Carnesecchi was condemned to death. How will the Lord of the Church have judged His servant, who dared, as His Vicar upon earth, to condemn doctrines which may almost all of them be traced back as utterances of Christ or of His Apostles? Nevertheless, the wisdom and moderation with which Carnesecchi must have spoken upon all questionable points are admirable, and it seems marvellous that they did not blot out a tribunal so malevolent. To say anything more upon this judgment of the 'holy' Inquisition is unnecessary.

The no less hypocritical sentence itself we here give *verbatim* :—

'Taking into consideration the numerous deceptions practised upon the Holy Church, and the very many perjuries, inconstancies, fluctuations, and vacillations, and also thine inconsistencies and instability, how hard it has been for thee to confess the truth, and the impenitence which thou hast by many tokens manifested, and, amongst others, by writing to and counselling heretics even whilst in prison, and, as has been stated, thine inveterate career in error and in intercourse with heretics, and thine incorrigibility, since, on three other occasions besides this, sentence has been passed on thee and upon thy cause, and that thou hast in reference to them deluded and deceived the Holy Office; and that neither hast thou, after the two abovementioned absolutions, either amended or corrected thyself; taking which into consideration, the Holy Office can no longer trust thee, or have assurance that thou hast truly and sincerely repented, or may expect any amelioration on thy part;

'For this reason, we accordingly declare and adjudge that thou art an impenitent heretic, a dissembling convert, and debased; and that by the very law thou art deprived, and, so far as it is necessary, we do deprive thee anew, of every rank, privilege, and eminent position; and of thy preferments, emoluments, and occupations, ecclesiastical and secular, whatsoever they may be, and howsoever designated; and that they have ceased to be enjoyed by thee from the date of thy heresies; and that thenceforward thou wast incapable of obtaining them. And we condemn thee to the forfeiture of all thy property, personal and real, and of all consequent rights and claims, agreeably to the appointment of the sacred canon; to be applied, as we do apply it, to the purpose to which it should be justly assigned.

'And, as one irreclaimable, without remorse, and whose change of mind has only been fictitious, we in like manner pronounce and ordain, that thou oughtest to be degraded, as we direct, that thou be actually degraded, from the Orders which thou hast attained. And, as a person thus degraded, henceforward, as well now as previously, we expel thee as an unprofitable branch from our Ecclesiastical Court, and from the safeguard of our Holy Church, and we surrender and deliver thee up to the Secular Court; that is, to your Lordship the Governor of Rome, that you may take him under your jurisdiction; and that he may be subject to your decision; so as to be punished with due chastisement—beseeching you, however, as we do earnestly beseech you, so to mitigate the severity of your sentence in respect to his body, that there may be no danger either of death or of shedding of blood.

'So we, Cardinals Inquisitors-General, whose names are hereunder written, decree.

> 'BERNARDINO DI TRANI.
> 'SCIPOINE DI PISA.
> 'FRANCESCO PACHECO.
> 'GIOVANNI FRANCESCO DI GAMBARA.'

For a month and more had Carnesecchi to await his death, in that horrible prison, the Tor di Nona, whither he was now transported. Once more did the Duke Cosimo of Florence seek to save his former friend. He besought the Pope to be merciful; and execution was deferred. A Capuchin monk visited the prisoner in his cell, and announced to him that he might save his life if he would now adopt the faith of the Romish Church. But the monk himself was well nigh converted by Carnesecchi's spirited testimonies to his faith, and he returned to the person who had sent him, having achieved nothing.

Early on the morning of October 3rd, 1567, a scaffold was erected on the Ponte St. Angelo. He who had been at one time Papal Protonotary, and who by birth was a member of a patrician family, was not to be hanged, but beheaded; his body was then to be committed to the flames.

Carnesecchi retained his composure and strength of faith until the last moment. They dressed him in a *sanbenito*, an heretical garb, painted over with flames and devils; but he insisted that he would at least appear in clean linen. He wore a white shirt, he had a new pair of gloves, and a white handkerchief in his hand.

His noble head fell, whilst he was the object of the execrations and curses of those who held themselves to be members of that Church which exclusively arrogates salvation to them who are within its pale. And whilst the ashes to which his body was reduced were cast into the Tiber, his soul was with his Lord; for he was faithful unto death, and received the crown of life.

www.ingramcontent.com/pod-product-compliance
Lightning Source LLC
Chambersburg PA
CBHW020307090426
42735CB00009B/1253